IMAGES
of England

THE KING'S OWN
YORKSHIRE
LIGHT INFANTRY
1857-1968

Her Majesty Queen Elizabeth, The Queen Mother, Colonel-in-Chief of The King's Own Yorkshire Light Infantry.

IMAGES
of England

THE KING'S OWN YORKSHIRE LIGHT INFANTRY 1857-1968

Compiled by
Malcolm K. Johnson
for the King's Own Yorkshire Light Infantry

TEMPUS

First published 2000
Copyright © The King's Own Yorkshire Light Infantry, 2000

Tempus Publishing Limited
The Mill, Brimscombe Port,
Stroud, Gloucestershire, GL5 2QG

ISBN 0 7524 1867 X

Typesetting and origination by
Tempus Publishing Limited
Printed in Great Britain by
Midway Clark Printing, Wiltshire

Commissioned into the 51st Foot in 1775 at the age of fourteen and a half, Sir John Moore (1761-1809) commanded the Regiment in 1790. At the siege of Calvi, Corsica (1794), the Grenadier and right companies (including the 51st) of Sir Charles Stuart's Expeditionary Force were commanded by Moore. During the siege a cannon ball struck the ground nearby and flying gravel from the impact destroyed the sight in the right eye of Capt. Horatio Nelson, who was standing next to him. Sir John Moore was killed on 16 January 1809 at the Battle of Corunna while commanding the British forces fighting Napoleon's Army in northern Spain.

Contents

During the Peninsular War the 51st took part in the siege of Badajos, June 1811. Ensign Joseph Dyas volunteered to lead 'The Forlorn Hope' – the first group to storm the walls immediately after the bombardment and ahead of the main assault. The first attempt was unsuccessful, but Dyas led a second and a third attempt, and would have led a fourth had it been ordered. From that time onwards the Regimental Toast, drunk in silence, on every band night in the officers mess was 'Dyas and the Stormers'. He died at Ballymena in 1850.

Lieutenant-General Archibald Brown-Dyce began his military career as a Cadet in the Madras Army in 1816 and became an Ensign the following year. At Arnee, in 1839, he raised the 2nd Madras European Light Infantry, a regiment which became part of the Honourable East India Company's forces. He rose to the rank of Lt-Gen. in 1860 and was appointed Colonel of the 2nd Madras LI when it was renumbered the 105th in 1861. He served the whole of his career in India, China and Burma and died on 9 March 1866.

Introduction

On 27 December 1755 the second Marquis of Rockingham, Lord Lieutenant of the West Riding of Yorkshire, and Sir George Saville received warrants for recruiting men to a new regiment. Thus, shortly after a public meeting held in Leeds on 16 March 1756, recruiting to the 53rd Regiment of Foot was completed. Two years later a reorganization resulted in the Regiment being renumbered the 51st Foot. On 1 August 1759 the 51st took part in the Battle of Minden, one of the many battles of the Seven Years War (1756-63). The battle is chiefly remembered for the exploits of the 51st who, together with five other regiments of the British Brigade (The 'Unsurpassable Six' as Thomas Carlyle called them), drove off a French cavalry charge with musket fire. They then routed the centre of the French infantry at the point of the bayonet. After the battle the men picked white roses, found growing near the battlefield, and put them in their hats – a tradition which was carried on by the regiments every 1 August from then onwards. (Today Yorkshire Day is celebrated on 1 August.)

The 51st was part of Wellington's army in the Peninsular during the Napoleonic Wars and was present at the Battle of Waterloo occupying a position near Hougoumont Farm from where it had the distinction of firing the first shots of the battle on 18 June 1815. In the nineteenth century the Regiment served mainly in India, the North-West Frontier and Burma. In the army reforms of 1881 the 51st was paired with the 105th Madras European Light Infantry to form, respectively, the 1st and 2nd Battalion, the King's Own Light Infantry (South Yorkshire Regiment). A further change of name in 1888 produced the King's Own Yorkshire Light Infantry (KOYLI).

The 2nd Battalion KOYLI was involved in the Boer War at the turn of the century, and many veterans of that conflict were to be found in the ranks of the twenty-six Battalions which the Regiment raised for service in the First World War. Battalions of the KOYLI saw action on the Western Front, Italy, Salonika and Egypt winning six Victoria Crosses and 1,347 other gallantry awards.

In 1927 King George V honoured the King's Own Yorkshire Light Infantry when he appointed Her Majesty Queen Elizabeth the Queen Mother, then Duchess of York, its Colonel-in-Chief. The Regiment is duly proud of its association with Her Majesty and is most grateful to her for the deep personal interest which she has shown in its activities for over seventy years.

Further service abroad followed and on the outbreak of the Second World War the 1st KOYLI went to France, while the 2nd Battalion was in Burma. The territorial battalions, the 1/4, 2/4, served with distinction in North Africa, Italy and North-West Europe. Other battalions of the Regiment were converted to regiments of the Royal Artillery while the 7th became a regiment of the Royal Armoured Corps and fought at Kohima and Imphal in 1944. At the end of the war the KOYLI was reduced to one regular battalion and further reforms in 1968 saw the amalgamation of all light infantry regiments into the Light Infantry, the KOYLI forming its second battalion.

It was not until the turn of the century that there are what may be called action photographs, and even here examples are few. The Boer War produced the first example of the KOYLI in action and more were to follow from the two World Wars. The Second World War provided lots of material, but as the photographers got closer to the action, strict censorship obliterated many identification badges, especially shoulder flashes. The photographs of the 2nd KOYLI in Burma in 1942 may appear indistinct, but the fact that they exist at all is quite remarkable. Sadly many post-1945 photographs were taken without accurate records being kept of dates, locations and names. It must be admitted that some photographs are of doubtful quality, especially those prior to 1900, but they have been included because they are the best available examples from specific periods or events.

Leaving aside the Regiment's history before the development of photography, a collection of over 200 photographs cannot possibly do justice to the period in question, especially if one considers the momentous events of the first half of the twentieth century. I hope the collection will prove of interest to those who have served in the Regiment, those who have had family connections in the past, and those who have a general interest in military history and the British Army in particular.

Malcolm K. Johnson
Doncaster 1999

Acknowledgements

Most of the photographs are taken from the archive of the King's Own Yorkshire Light Infantry. Examples labelled IWM are reproduced by courtesy of the Imperial War Museum; those labelled NAC are included by kind permission of the National Archive of Canada. *The Yorkshire Post*, *Sheffield Star*, *Wakefield Express* and Doncaster Central Library have generously contributed material from their archives. Lt-Col. G. Barker-Harland and Richard Todd loaned examples from the Second World War; John Scurr and Eddie Robinson providing some of the Malayan ones. Many examples from the Regimental Journal *The Bugle*, were taken by the Army Public Relations Department, but unfortunately the originals have proved impossible to locate. I would like to thank all those who have assisted in the compilation of this collection, especially Major C.M.J. Deedes the Regimental Secretary, his predecessor Col J.S. Cowley and Mr G. Preece and the staff of the Doncaster Metropolitan Borough Museum.

One
1857-1914

Following two years of hard fighting in the Second Burma War (1852-54), the 51st King's Own Light Infantry left for Malta (their ultimate destination being the Crimea) in June 1855. The end of the Crimean War changed this plan and in May 1856 the Regiment sailed for England, and then a move to the Curragh, near Dublin (often referred to as the Aldershot of Ireland) where this photograph was taken in 1857.

This bell, weighing 6cwt, was taken from the Great Pagoda after the capture of Rangoon, 1852, and was brought back to England and presented to the city of York by Capt. A.H. Irby. In September 1853 the 51st was granted the battle honour of 'Pegu' in commemoration 'of the service rendered'.

Lt William Baillie took part in the Second Burma War and retired from the army shortly afterwards. Lt Baillie was the nephew of Lt-Col. William Baillie, commander of the Grenadier Company of the 51st Foot at the Battle of Minden in 1759.

As a junior officer Lt-Col. A.H. Irby fought in the Burma War and later commanded the 51st between 1857 and 1861. On the outbreak of the Indian Mutiny the 51st volunteered to return to India and arrived there 1 January 1858. Lt-Col. Irby died at Lahore in the cholera outbreak of 1861 in which the 51st suffered 288 dead, including 16 women and 16 children.

The Band of the 51st KOLI, India, 1865. The regimental history records that, in 1823 when it numbered one sergeant and fourteen musicians, 'The Band had not hitherto been taken very seriously by the Powers that be.'

Officers and NCOs of the 51st at the Citadel Barracks, Dover, April 1867. Capt. Burnaby, seated centre with swagger stick, later commanded the 51st from 1882 to 1887. Sergeants in Light Infantry regiments, back row centre, were allowed to wear chevrons on both arms.

The peakless caps, worn by the two colour sergeants of the 51st on the left, standing, were introduced in 1861. Minor changes in uniform were constantly being made in the nineteenth century. This photograph was taken at Winchester, 1867.

The 105th Madras European Light Infantry on parade at Meerut, India, in 1869, sometime after its arrival from Dinapore. Formed in 1839 as the 2nd Madras European Light Infantry, it served in many parts of India and Burma. After the Indian Mutiny (1856-58), in which the 105th took no part, those regiments raised and financed by the Honourable East India Company were absorbed into the British Army. On 10 April 1861 the 2nd Madras Light Infantry was renumbered 105th and appeared for the first time in the list of regiments of the British Army for 1863/64. At this time the Regiment was commanded by Lt-Col. J.R. Mackenzie, who retired with the rank of Maj.-Gen. in 1875.

Lt-Col. Mackenzie and officers of the 105th at Dinapore, Bengal, December 1868, a few weeks before the 105th moved to Meerut, India.

NCOs of the 105th at Meerut, 1869. Their relaxed appearance contrasts well with many of the more formal group photographs of the time.

Prior to the Crimean War the wearing of whiskers had been forbidden, but following that conflict, when many men had grown beards for protection against the extreme cold, the rules were relaxed and some of these men of 'A' Company of the 105th at Meerut, 1869, have taken full advantage.

The 51st returned to India in November 1872 and was stationed in Fyzabad for three years, where this photograph of 'A' Company was taken in 1874. They too are sporting some fine whiskers.

At the opening of the Second Afghan War (1878-80) the 51st formed part of the Peshawar Valley Field Force, one of the three columns which invaded Afghanistan under the command of Sir Frederick Roberts (later Lord Roberts). The Peshawar Column, commanded by Lt-Gen. Sir Samuel Browne, was to seize the Khyber Pass. Col. S.A. Madden (centre row holding long lance) and his officers relax after capturing the fort of Ali Musjid, 21 November 1878. The Regiment was awarded Afghanistan as one of its Battle Honours. These officers are wearing a variety of service uniforms.

Officers of the 51st, some wearing the Second Afghan War Medal, at Bareilly, India, 1883. The mixture of civilian clothes and uniforms suggests an informal rather than a regimental photograph.

NCOs of the 51st at Bareilly, in 1883, wearing the Second Afghan War Medal with the Ali Musjid Clasp. Those with two medals have the India General Service Medal with the Jowaki Clasp, awarded after the Jawaki Campaign of 1877/78. (Curiously the campaign is called Jawaki, but the clasp Jowaki.)

In November 1872 the 105th was sent to Aden, to deal with a little local difficulty, and remained there until February 1874 when it embarked for its first tour of home service. After periods in Sheffield, Colchester and the Channel Islands the Battalion was sent to Ireland in 1879. These officers, in Cork in 1880, exchanged these cap badges the following year when the army reforms linked the 51st KOLI with the 105th Madras LI to create the 1st and 2nd battalions of the King's Own Light Infantry (South Yorkshire Regiment).

The 1st KOLI formed up in square at Dinapore, 1885. Originally used by infantry to repel cavalry, this formation was useful against enemies in superior numbers, but armed with primitive weapons.

Officers and senior NCOs of the 1st KOLI during the Third Burma War. The war began in November 1885 and ended in January 1886, but a guerrilla war, in which the 1st KOLI was involved, carried on until 1887.

Originally thought to have been a patrol of the 1st KOYLI, this photograph shows artillerymen (wearing swords), not infantrymen. During the war in Burma, two guns of the Royal Artillery, plus 100 Bengal Sappers and Miners, did accompany the 1st KOLI on the Ruby Mines Expedition, November 1886, and these could be those guns.

Senior NCOs near their barracks at Mandalay, Burma, November 1887. The Battalion had been here in October of the previous year, but on each occasion their stay only lasted two or three days.

Sgt Albert Green of the 51st King's Own Light Infantry was born 23 August 1841 and enlisted in the 51st KOLI on 30 April 1856. He was Bandmaster from 1868 to 1888 and married the daughter of Col.-Sgt James Murray, also of the 51st, on 17 August 1868. On his retirement from the army he became a Yeoman Warder of the Tower of London from 16 January 1888. Sgt Green died on 19 March 1898. He is pictured here wearing the India General Service Medal (1854-95).

'H' Company, 2nd KOYLI, wearing Glengarry caps at Quetta, India, 1888. From 1887 onwards the Regiment was known as the King's Own Yorkshire Light Infantry (KOYLI).

The Regimental silver of the 2nd KOYLI on display in the officers mess at Quetta, 1888. Much of this silver was lost in the retreat to Imphal in 1942.

The 1st KOYLI returned to England in December 1887 and almost thirty years of peacetime soldiering. After one year at Gosport, and two years in Guernsey and Alderney, the Battalion moved to Belfast in June 1893.

BELFAST, 1893.

Lieut.M.N.K.Connolly.

'THE RETREAT', WILLOW BANK BARRACKS, BELFAST, CHRISTMAS 1893

Half the Battalion was stationed at Victoria Barracks, the rest were at Willow Bank Barracks where the sounding of retreat was photographed at Christmas 1893.

Officers of the 2nd KOYLI who took part in The Tirah Expedition, (Afghanistan). In a day-long battle in the Shin Kamar Pass, 29 January 1898, the Battalion lost three officers and twenty-seven men killed, three officers and thirty-one men wounded.

Two Buglers of the 2nd KOYLI with a donkey they captured during the Tirah Expedition. The Battalion returned to Ahmednagar in April 1898 where this photograph was taken.

The 2nd KOYLI soccer team in Poona, 1899, was rarely able to play against the 1st KOYLI team since one battalion was always on foreign service while the other was on home service.

From Belfast the 1st KOYLI moved to Dublin on 4 August 1897. Competitive sports included the tug-o-war and this 1899 team is displaying some of their training equipment – and a suitably determined look.

Physical training was a regular part of a soldier's life and these men of the 1st KOYLI are carrying out a knees bend exercise with no apparent discomfort.

Route marches kept the men fit and hardened their feet. Men of the 1st KOYLI are seen here resting in sand dunes before continuing the march back to their barracks in Dublin sometime in 1899.

A series of photographs of the 1st KOYLI was taken on 26 March 1899 at the Beggar's Bush Barracks, Dublin, to mark the completion of Lt-Col. G.P.F. Byng's period of command. The Colonel is seen here, front row centre, with the officers of the battalion.

The Regimental Band of the 1st KOYLI at Beggar's Bush Barracks. A well-appointed and competent band was needed not only for the parade ground, but also for social functions, especially when stationed abroad.

A Maxim machine-gun and six riflemen of the 1st KOYLI at Beggar's Bush Barracks. Invented by Sir Hiram Maxim, between 1883 and 1885, the gun was adopted by the British army in 1888. It was capable of firing a complete 250 round belt in one minute and was powerful enough to halt a whole battalion, given a good field of fire. In 1891 Lt-Col. Symons, commanding the 2nd KOYLI, bought a .45 calibre Maxim and presented it to the Battalion. It was used on the Isazai Expedition of 1892; the first recorded use of the Maxim with troops on field service in India. By 1914 the wheels and carriage had been replaced by a stand, which meant the machine-gun team had to carry it over difficult terrain.

In March 1899 half the 2nd KOYLI went to Mauritius, the remainder to South Africa. The Boer war began in October and by November the whole battalion had taken part in the Battle of Modder River. This memorial was erected soon after the battle.

In South Africa infantry battalions formed mounted companies. Lt Ottley, front row, second from the right, commanded the 2nd KOYLI company and is seen with 2Lt R.F. Riley and the NCOs at Wynberg near Cape Town.

As the army moved through South Africa many rivers and streams had to be crossed. This transport section wagon of the 2nd KOYLI was stuck in the mud while crossing Rhenoster Drift.

Following their efforts to cross Rhenoster Drift the Battalion is seen taking a well-earned rest before renewing the march.

The 3rd Mounted Infantry (2nd KOYLI) outside a blockhouse, probably near Ermelo. Capt. Thorold, second from the left, middle row, and Lt Brooke, fourth from the right, back row, were both killed in an action at Bakenlaagte, near Ermelo, 30 October 1900. Lt Brewis, second from the left, back row, was captured but later escaped.

Piquet formed by 'C' Company, 2nd KOYLI, on the Magaliesburg Range, December 1900. Their camp was attacked and these positions had to be vacated. In the action the battalion lost seven men killed and fourteen wounded.

The 1st KOYLI Mounted Infantry Company at the Curragh, February 1901. Commanded by Capt. A.S. Colquhoun and including Lt C.P. Deedes and Lt C.F.B. Powell, it arrived in South Africa, on 7 April, and went to Pretoria.

In South Africa General French often referred to the 2nd KOYLI as his 'foot cavalry', and if, as Napoleon said, 'an army marches on its stomach', then these battalion cooks and butchers deserved some of the credit.

Count Roberto Zileri dal Verme, the civilian in the centre, was big game hunting in South Africa when war broke out. He joined the 2nd KOYLI and was later awarded an honorary DSO, one of only three civilians ever to be given the award – the other two being royal princes.

At the end of the Boer War the 2nd KOYLI left South Africa for Malta where the Governor, Lord Grenfell, presented the officers and men with the King's South African Medal, 9 February 1903.

The 1st KOYLI at Limerick, Ireland, 1 August 1900. Two weeks later HRH the Duke of Connaught inspected the battalion and reported, 'The 1st Battalion KOYLI is composed of a fine body of soldier-like men with efficient officers.'

This recruiting poster refers to annual training which, in 1903, took place at Edale Camp, Derbyshire. The strength of the 3rd KOYLI at this time was 19 officers and 783 men.

The 2nd KOYLI left Malta and spent 1904 in Crete. It returned to Sheffield in March 1905, where it was presented with new colours by King Edward VII on 12 July 1905.

The old colours of the 2nd KOYLI, dating from 1868, were placed in York Minster on 20 June 1906. The Band, Buglers and a Guard of Honour are formed up at York station before marching to the Minster for the ceremony.

Signallers of the 1st KOYLI when stationed at Gibraltar, 1905. Flags, heliographs, lamps and long telescopes seem to be their main equipment.

Men of the 2nd KOYLI Cycle Company were equipped with sturdy machines in 1900. These early 'mechanized troops' may have found cross-country riding rather difficult.

The Regimental Barracks in Pontefract, 1908. Minden House, the former sergeant's mess, is all that remains and houses the Regimental and Light Infantry Office for Yorkshire. The word 'Me' can just be seen below the guard.

Private Singleton with his kit neatly laid out in one of the barrack blocks, c. 1908.

HORSE DRAWN TRANSPORT, ABOUT 1909

When a battalion moved the men marched and their ammunition, stores and extra equipment were carried by the horse drawn transport section. This transport section of 1909 belonged to the 2nd KOYLI.

Some of the families also accompanied the Battalion: officers and ladies of the 1st KOYLI in South Africa, c. 1907. A variety of uniforms are seen here, the darker khaki, worn by Capt. C.P. Deedes, fourth from the left, middle row, was to become familiar during the First World War.

The Haldane Reforms of 1908 produced the Territorial Army. Territorial battalions conducted annual camps and the 5th KOYLI camp in 1908 took place at Redcar.

On reaching establishment, Territorial battalions were allowed to carry colours; the 5th KOYLI received theirs from King Edward VII. The colour party is seen here at Doncaster station following the ceremony at Windsor Castle on 26 June 1909.

Sometimes the annual camp was a great distance away. The 5th KOYLI are seen parading shortly after their arrival on the Isle of Man in 1910.

Route marches were a regular chore for the infantrymen. These officers and men of 'F' Company, 2nd KOYLI, are moving with 'casual ease' along a country road somewhere near Aldershot, 1910.

The 1st KOYLI drawn up on parade in Cape Town to hear the proclamation of the accession to the throne of King George V on 6 May 1910.

The 5th KOYLI firing a *Feu de Joie* in Glasgow Paddocks, Doncaster, on Coronation Day, 22 June 1911. The rifles were discharged in sequence, not in a volley, which accounts for the smoke in different parts of the line.

Signallers of the 1st KOYLI in Singapore, 1913. CSM Skilton, seated centre, returned to England in 1914 and transferred to the 6th (Service) Battalion, KOYLI, one of the first Kitchener battalions to see active service.

The first decade of the twentieth century saw the importation from the USA of a new style of popular music. This is the 2nd KOYLI's Ragtime Band of 1913.

Two
1914-1918

For Great Britain and the Empire the First World War began on Tuesday 4 August 1914. 'A' Company of the 2nd KOYLI are seen here on a route march from Portobello Barracks, Dublin, on the day before war was declared.

Officers of the 2nd KOYLI shortly after their arrival in France. On 23 August the Battalion was near the Belgium town of Mons, awaiting the arrival of the advancing Germans. Despite superior rifle skill the British Expeditionary Force (BEF) was forced to retreat by the sheer weight of enemy numbers. On 26 August the II Corps (which included the 2nd KOYLI) turned to face the enemy at Le Cateau and held them for a whole day, but when orders to retire were issued they failed to reach the 2nd KOYLI who were overwhelmed. The Battalion left England with 850 officers and men; by midnight, 26 August, it had lost 18 officers, 21 sergeants, 22 corporals, 7 buglers and 532 privates. Following the action, Maj. Yates and L/Cpl Holmes were awarded the VC.

Maj. C.A.L. Yates VC, 2nd KOYLI, was captured at Le Cateau. He was killed while attempting to escape from the prisoner of war camp at Torgau and is buried in the town's cemetery.

All the officers captured at Le Cateau were imprisoned at Torgau. They agreed to contribute to a German Red Cross charity, each signing this cheque on the back which was then sent to England for clearance. In this way their families discovered they were alive.

In August 1914
the 1st KOYLI was
stationed in
Singapore.
Ordered home in
September they
left from Borneo
Wharf, Singapore,
aboard the S.S.
Carnarvonshire.

Officers of the 1st KOYLI with some of
the *Carnarvonshire*'s officers as they
returned to England and eventual
involvement on the Western Front.

When war was declared in 1914, the Regiment's territorial battalions, 4th and 5th, were at their annual camp. They immediately returned from Whitby to their home depots of Wakefield and Doncaster.

Kitchener's famous appeal raised many new battalions. These men of the 12th KOYLI, training at Otley, are wearing the blue uniforms which many battalions wore before receiving the official khaki. (Courtesy of *Yorkshire Post*)

Pte Marshall, who enlisted in 1915, looks particularly young to be exposed to the horrors of the Western Front.

Pte Gilbert Jarman was posted to the 5th KOYLI in France, March 1918, and was wounded at Havrincourt, September 1918. Here, aged one hundred and one, he displays the French Légion d'Honneur which he received, on 29 October 1999, from the Honorary French Consul at a ceremony in Wakefield Town Hall. (Courtesy of *Wakefield Express*)

The new battalions were given training in musketry, bayonet fighting and, of course, route marches. The 1/4 KOYLI in shirtsleeve order on a route march somewhere in southern England, 1915.

Officers of 'D' Company, 6th (Service) Battalion KOYLI, in September 1914. Left to right, back row: Lt W.F. Burrows, 2Lt C. Leatham, 2Lt K. Musgrave (KIA). Front row: Capt. W.N. Tempest (KIA), Capt. E.B. Wilson, Lt R. Anne (KIA).

Cpl Lappin, 1/5th KOYLI, winning the DCM near Ypres, 27 October 1915. The official citation reads: 'At 9.20 am he proceeded on his own initiative and unaccompanied, to make a reconnaissance of the enemy's trenches. He went over our parapet and crawled across the intervening space and under the German's barbed wire to their parapet. He looked through a small breach in their parapet and obtained valuable information as to the condition of the trenches and the strength in which they were held, and successfully returned with the desired intelligence. On 29 October Corporal Lappin again went over the parapet in broad daylight and crawled to the Bulgarian flag fixed by the Germans about 80 yards from our trenches and 30 yards from their own and brought it, with its nine-foot pole, safely back to our trenches under heavy rifle fire.' (Artist – W.S. Bagdatopulos)

These signallers of the 2/4 KOYLI would use both wireless and telephones, neither displayed here, but both were quite primitive in a war where lack of good communications was to cost thousands of lives.

Away from the line often meant fetching and carrying for others. Relaxation did occur sometimes and hopefully these men of the 2nd KOYLI had a chance to see the film at their local cinema, 1916.

Capt. W.J. Tempest, wounded near Ypres in 1915 while serving with the 6th KOYLI, transferred to the Royal Flying Corps (RFC) and became the second pilot to shoot down a German Zeppelin over England. He was awarded the DSO for destroying the Zeppelin L31 over Potters Bar, 1 October 1916. (IWM)

Some infantry battalions collected money to buy aeroplanes for the RFC. This Sopwith Camel fighter, one of three aircraft bought by the regiment, was paid for by the 3rd KOYLI, the reserve battalion stationed permanently in England.

A series of photographs were taken on 1 October 1917 in the village of Weiltje near Ypres, during the Third Battle of Ypres (Passchendaele). Ypres, usually associated with mud, could be dry, but even so each rifle has a cover to protect the bolt and magazine. (IWM)

These men at Weiltje relax with a game of cards. The Regimental light infantry bugle can just be made out on the shirt of the man on the right with the balding head. (IWM)

The cooks in charge of the Battalion's field kitchen in Weiltje appear to have chosen a good site. A relaxed atmosphere seems to be accompanying the proceedings, even though the front line is only a few miles up the road. (IWM)

The KOYLI Trench Mortar Company in Weiltje inserting fuses into their Stokes trench mortar ammunition. With so much live ammunition nearby this task needed extreme care. (IWM)

In July 1918, the 2/4 and 5th KOYLI (62nd Division) moved to the Marne area to reinforce the French Army. KOYLI officers confer with their French and Italian counterparts before the battle of Tardenois, 20 July 1918. (IWM)

Once the plans are finalized, of course, the officers get down to the more pleasurable activity of hospitality in the alfresco surroundings. (IWM)

A KOYLI soldier (2/4 or 5th Battalion) in the woods of the Chateau de Commetreuil on the first day of the Battle of Tardenois, the first in a series of remarkable Allied successes during the final 100 days of the war. (IWM)

Men of the 5th KOYLI examining debris in a captured German position during the battle of Tardenois. Certain follow-up troops collected enemy papers, maps, photographs and personal letters to pass on to the Intelligence Officers for analysis. (IWM)

The 51st Graduation Battalion of the KOYLI at Welbeck Camp in late 1918. These battalions of conscripts supplied reinforcements to the various KOYLI battalions on the Western Front.

The war ended at 11a.m. on 11 November 1918 and within days a colour party of the 5th KOYLI arrived in Doncaster from France to collect their colours which had been left in the safe keeping of the Mayor.

The 9,447 men of the King's Own Yorkshire Light Infantry who lost their lives during the war are here represented by 40515 Pte W.E. Spence, 10th KOYLI, killed in action, 6 January 1918.

A wreath of poppies laid by members of the KOYLI Regimental Association at the Menin Gate Memorial, Ypres, August 1993.

Three

1918-1939

The 1st KOYLI went to France in January 1915 but was later sent to Salonika. The Battalion returned to France in late 1918 and are seen here parading their colour in the town square of Bavai in Belgium, 13 May 1919.

The 1st KOYLI returned to Germany as part of the Army of Occupation in 1922. The Battalion was divided with two companies stationed on the eastern border in Oppeln, Silesia, while the remainder were in Cologne on the western border. After only a few months the Oppeln detachment moved to Cologne where this photograph was taken of the whole Battalion being inspected by the C-in-C British Forces Germany. The partitioning of Silesia by the Treaty of Versailles in 1919, (part going to Poland and part to the newly created state of Czechoslovakia) was to be a contributory cause of the Second World War.

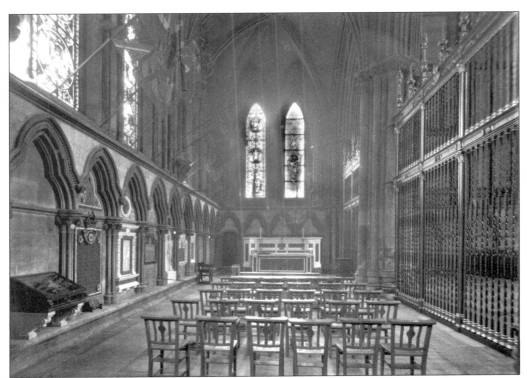

The Regimental Chapel in York Minster saw numerous ceremonies in the early 1920s as memorial services were held to commemorate those who had been killed in the First World War.

REMEMBER·BEFORE·GOD
THE·9447·OF·ALL·RANKS
OF·THE·KING'S·OWN✠
YORKSHIRE·LIGHT✠✠
INFANTRY·WHO·GAVE
THEIR·LIVES·IN·THE
GREAT·WAR·1914-1919
WHOSE·NAMES·ARE
INSCRIBED·IN·THE✠
BOOK·OF·REMEMBRANCE
LAID·UP·IN·THIS·MINSTER
CEDE·NULLIS

This inscription was placed in the Regiment's Memorial Chapel, York Minster, 1 August 1922.

In 1922 the 2nd KOYLI were at Ferozepore, India. In this colour party are, left to right: Cpl Drury, Lt M.G. Beckett, Sgt L. Calvert VC MM (awarded the VC for gallantry at Havrincourt with the 5th KOYLI, September 1918), 2Lt H.A. Livock, Cpl Podel.

The colour party of the 1st KOYLI leaving Buckingham Palace after being presented with new colours by King George V, 5 July 1926. Left to right: an unknown civilian, RSM Crossland, Sgt Routledge DCM MM, Cpl Fox MM (obscured), L/Cpl Tyler, 2Lt Hon. P. Hotham, -?-, Bt Lt-Col. M.F. Day MC, 2Lt J.W.R. Dugmore, -?- (obscured).

In 1927 King George V honoured the King's Own Yorkshire Light Infantry by appointing Her Royal Highness, The Duchess of York, Colonel-in-Chief of the Regiment.

HER ROYAL HIGHNESS THE DUCHESS OF YORK.
COLONEL-IN-CHIEF,
THE KING'S OWN YORKSHIRE LIGHT INFANTRY.

Most Humbly submitted to Your Majesty
by Your Majesty's Most Humble
and Most Devoted Servant.

App^d
G.R.I.

That Her Royal Highness The Duchess
of York, be appointed Colonel-in-Chief,
The King's Own Yorkshire Light Infantry.

The War Office.
4 August 1927

The Letter of Appointment.

The new Colonel-in-Chief
inspected the 1st KOYLI at
Blackdown Camp, 15 December
1927. The Duchess, seen here
inspecting the men, was escorted
by the Battalion's commanding
officer Lt-Col. A.R. Keppel.

The visit of the Duchess involved
more than inspecting lines of men
on parade and the Sergeants Mess
was only one area over which she
cast a critical eye.

The Royal Hospital, Chelsea, Easter 1928. Left to right, back row: Albert Cape (51st: 1877-85), W.S. Mills (105th: 1878-96), M. Henry (51st: 1877-84), M. Carroll (2nd KOYLI: 1895-1902). Front row: W. Oliver (51st: 1871-76), W.L. Wilson (51st: 1870-82), J.E. Gadsby (105th: 1878-90). All saw active service in Afghanistan except Gadsby who was invalided home after service in the Boer War.

Minden Day 1928 was celebrated at York, and was the first occasion the new Colonel-in-Chief was able to present white roses to the KOYLI.

The CO of the 4th KOYLI, Bt-Col. F.H.T. Cartwright (front row, centre) and his staff at the 1928 camp held at Beverley. Among this dazzling array of medals gained during the First World War are: one DSO, two MCs, two DCMs and one MM.

A TERRITORIAL BATTALION AT CAMP, ABOUT 1925

Not all Territorial camps took place in fine weather. For men who had experienced the dire conditions on the Western Front this amount of rain and mud was of little consequence.

In 1932 the 2nd KOYLI were back on the North-West Frontier of India. The Battalion is leaving the parade after trooping their colour in Peshawar, now part of Pakistan.

Maj. T.B. Butt (centre left) and Lt B.W. Wood, with the 2nd KOYLI's Indian Platoon in Peshawar, 1932. Between the wars most battalions had an Indian platoon, but after 1938 the Indian troops were absorbed into the Indian Army regiments.

Following a ceremony, in 1933, to dedicate two windows in York Minster to the dead of the First World War, Her Royal Highness, the Colonel-in-Chief left the Minster. She is seen escorted by Lt-Col. L.B. Daly, commanding 1st KOYLI on the left, and Major-Gen Sir Charles Deedes, Colonel of the Regiment, on the right.

The 1st KOYLI at their Blackdown Camp in 1933. These small lightly armoured machine-gun carriers (Carden-Lloyd Carriers) were the fore-runners of the larger Bren-Gun carriers of the Second World War.

Gibraltar was always a popular posting and the 1st KOYLI machine-gun company, commanded by Lt C.J. Deedes, are seen displaying a selection of their armoury, December 1936.

The Coronation of King George VI took place on 21 May 1937 and The King's Own Yorkshire Light Infantry's Colonel-in-Chief now became Queen Elizabeth. A contingent from the 1st KOYLI is seen here in the Coronation Parade.

In 1936 the 2nd KOYLI moved to Maymyo near Mandalay, Burma. The escort for the Burma Boundary Commission was provided by 'A' Company, and one section of 'S' Company, pictured here on parade.

LADIES MATCH SHOOT					
2ND Bn KOYLI V 1st Bn KOYLI					
NAMES	1	2	3	4	TOTAL
MRS BUTT	25	16	14	15	70
MRS WILKINSON	25	13	16	12	66
MRS HOTHAM	25	20	20	6	71
MRS FORBES	25	13	16	15	69
MRS VALLANCE	20	12	17	12	61
MRS WRIDE	25	18	15	9	67
MRS BRAYSON	25	9	10	6	50
MISS THOMAS	25	18	14	15	72
				GRAND TOTAL	526

The ladies' rifle team from the 2nd KOYLI narrowly lost the annual competition with the ladies of the 1st KOYLI by one point in 1937.

After three years in Gibraltar the 1st KOYLI returned to the new barracks at Strensall, York, where these men were photographed cleaning their rifles and equipment in 1938.

A patrol of the 2nd KOYLI, under the command of Lt Quiney, in the streets of Rangoon during the serious rioting which took place between Moslem and Hindu Indians and the Buddhist Burmese, 26 July 1938.

In 1939, as Europe prepared once more for war, the 2nd KOYLI returned to Maymyo where this photograph of No. 15 Platoon, 'D' Company, was taken.

The 2nd KOYLI's machine-gun company at Maymyo. These guns were taken from the Battalion just before it went to war in January 1942 and were given to a Burmese unit for airfield defence. It is believed they were never used.

Four
1939-1945

The 1st KOYLI crossed to France on 4 October 1939 and immediately began to prepare defensive positions near Douai close to the Belgian border. After two weeks in trenches near Metz it moved to Bondeau, near Lille, where it passed the harsh winter of 1939/40 training and waiting during the period of inactivity known as the 'Phoney War'. A break for a smoke was always welcome. Note that Bren-guns have now replaced the Vickers machine-guns seen in Carden-Lloyd carriers of 1933. (IWM)

This Bren-gun practice in Bondeau seems to be taking place in someone's back garden. (IWM)

In April 1940 the 5th Infantry Division (including the 1st KOYLI) was sent to help the Norwegians resist the German invasion. The Battalion was ordered to leave its Bren-gun carriers, and much of its transport, behind in France. (IWM)

The 1/4 KOYLI (49th West Riding Division) had been sent to Norway earlier. This painting, by Maj. J.R. Dugmore commanding 'C' Company, depicts the Battalion's transports being bombed in Ran Fiord prior to disembarkation on 16 April 1940.

Leaving everything behind, except what each man could carry, the 1/4 KOYLI left Namsos aboard the liner El Jezair, shown here nearest to the pier on 3 May 1940. The following day the Battalion was safely back at Scapa Flow.

Five days after returning from Norway the 49th Division, including the 1/4 KOYLI, was sent to Iceland to prevent the Germans occupying the island. Capt. G.P. Roberts, and others in his company, test the springs of a Bren-gun carrier.

Accommodation was in the ubiquitous Nissen Hut. Capt. Roberts, seen here outside a typical example, was killed at Tessel Wood in Normandy on 25 June 1944.

The ski section of 'A' Company, 1/4 KOYLI, at Seydisfiord, Iceland, 1941. Their skiing skills were never put to the test in the North-West European campaign.

The ski section on patrol in Iceland, 1941. The only enemy forces they encountered were German reconnaissance aircraft, and they were usually flying far to high to be troubled by the Battalion's anti-aircraft guns. (IWM)

Extremely cold winters, short summers and inactivity characterized the stay in Iceland. 'C' Company constructed defensive positions near this picturesque hamlet of Eskifiordur on the island's east coast.

Capt. Richard Todd, third from the right, front row, left Iceland to command a signals course at Berwick before transferring to the 6th Airborne Division. He took part in the capture of Pegasus Bridge across the River Orne in the early hours of D-Day. His most famous screen role was that of Group Capt. Guy Gibson VC in the film *The Dam Busters*.

Arriving in France too late to have any real effect, the 2/4 KOYLI left via Cherbourg on 17 June 1940. In late 1940 (or early 1941) they were inspected by General Montgomery, seen here with Lt-Col. G.D. Ainger, centre, and Maj. G.H. Wilfor at their camp at Hythe. (IWM)

During his inspection of the 2/4 KOYLI at Hythe, General Montgomery stopped to talk to CSM Storey who is wearing the Shire Oak shoulder flash of the 46th Infantry Division. (IWM)

As the first British unit to go into action in Burma, the 2nd KOYLI took part in the retreat to Imphal, January to May 1942. Left to right: Maj. Martin, Lt-Col. Chadwick and another officer resting between Myingun and Yenangyaung on 16 April 1942. Martin was killed destroying a supply dump to prevent it falling into enemy hands.

Officers in the village of Taungtha on 25 April 1942. They are, left to right: a Chinese Captain, 2Lt R.E.S. Tanner, 2Lt J. Marsh and a corporal who was severely burned helping Major Martin to destroy the supply dump. The Chinese had attacked a Japanese road block at Yengangyaung and were returning to China.

Resting on a jungle trail on 9 May 1942.

Men and mules by the road side on 10 May. The survivors reached Imphal on 19 May, nine days after this photograph was taken. Only six officers and eighty-five men were left of the 2nd KOYLI. The Battalion returned to India to rebuild, but many survivors volunteered to serve with other groups, for instance, Brigadier Orde Wingate's Brigade (Chindits).

A number of KOYLI Battalions were converted from infantry to other branches of the army. The 7th KOYLI became the 149th Regiment of the Royal Armoured Corps and was sent to India in August 1941. Following extensive training in India throughout 1942 it saw action with the 2nd Division, its tanks being the first to relieve the garrison of Kohima. It went on to take part in the heavy fighting around Imphal, April and May 1944. This photograph of the regiment was taken in India.

The 5th KOYLI became the 53rd Light Ack Ack Regiment in November 1938. This Bofor gun's crew, in North Africa, consisted of, left to right: Gunners G. Ellis, ? Ayres, E. Otter, W. Coombs, G. Wiltshire, -?-, ? Bradley (on the other side of the bonnet).

In this street in Tripoli, in March 1943, the gun was temporarily put out of action (the breech was jammed by falling dirt) when a bomb exploded close by. The battery had been defending the port against an enemy air attack the previous night.

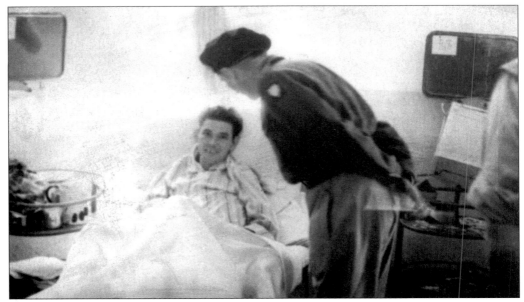

General Montgomery visited Gunner Robert Geddes, 170 Battery, 57th LAA Regiment in No. 2 General Hospital, Tripoli. The 57th LAA covered the 4th Indian Division, 8th Army, throughout the North African campaign. Gunner Geddes had been wounded at Wadi Akarit, 6 April 1943.

The 2/4 KOYLI, 46th Division, joined the First Army in North Africa landing at Algiers, 17 January 1943. CSM O'Pray MM briefs his men before a patrol. Some of the caps/hats are worn in a manner which appears to defy gravity. (IWM)

The 1st KOYLI was one of the first units to land in Sicily, 10 July 1943. Here they are advancing to attack Villasmundo, north-west of Augusta. In this action, known as 'The Battle of the Gorge', the Battalion lost a total of eight officers and eighty-eight other ranks. (IWM)

A patrol of the 1st KOYLI setting out towards Rionero, a village in the upper reaches of the Sangro River, Italy, in November 1943. The area was inhospitable and, despite the sunshine, it was obviously cold enough to require an overcoat. (IWM)

The 2/4 KOYLI rejoined the 8th Army on the Adriatic coast of Italy in July 1944. These men are dug in near Zollava during the battle for the Gemmano Ridge, south of Rimmini, in September 1944. (IWM)

The Yorkshire Dragoons (the last horsed cavalry of the British army) became the 9th KOYLI in February 1942. It served in North Africa and here at Coriano Ridge, north of the 2/4 KOYLI at Gemmano in September 1944. Shortly after this the 9th KOYLI was broken up, most joining the 2/4 KOYLI. (Courtesy of *Yorkshire Post*)

Following their return from Iceland, in August 1942, the 1/4 KOYLI eventually arrived in Lowestoft in December 1943. General Montgomery inspected the Battalion at Somerleyton Park, Suffolk. The Battalion landed in Normandy four days after D-Day. (IWM)

The village of Cristot in Normandy was attacked by the 1/4 KOYLI at noon on 16 June 1944. By evening it had been taken, but it was necessary to check that all the houses were clear of any surviving enemy. (IWM)

Cpl T. Waters, 5th Parachute Brigade, Signal section, won the Military Medal on the Caen Canal Bridge, Benouville, 6 June 1944. Cpl Waters joined the KOYLI in 1935 and served with the Regiment until 1943 when he volunteered for the newly formed Parachute Regiment. Following the airborne landing at Ranville on D-Day, it was vital to establish a telephone link between the 7th Parachute Battalion and its Brigade HQ. Cpl Waters, a wireless operator, was several hundred yards away from the bridge when he saw the linesmen under heavy fire. Without hesitation, and in full view of the enemy, he dashed out to rescue one of the wounded men. Then, calling for covering fire and throwing grenades himself, he ran onto the bridge, picked up the line layer, and in the face of heavy enemy fire succeeded in getting the line to the 7th Battalion HQ. (Artist – Peter Archer)

After heavy fighting around Caen, Lisieux and Le Havre, the 1/4 KOYLI moved north into Belgium. In Wuustwezel, north-east of Antwerp, Maj. A. Rutherfoord was given information about German positions by Josef Verellen on 21 October 1944.

This photograph of the two men on the same spot was taken forty-two years later when a party of 1/4 KOYLI veterans returned to the continent, in June 1986, to recreate their journey from Normandy to the Grebbe Line near Ede in Holland.

Pte Rain(centre) and Pte Turner (centre right) in Wuustwezel on 21 October 1944. Two men watching, while Pte Turner 'digs-in', would seem to be a satisfactory division of labour. (IWM)

Albert Richardson, standard bearer of the Wakefield Branch of the KOYLI Regimental Association, and L/Cpl Neil Hartshorne, a bugler from the 2nd Battalion Light Infantry, at the 49th Division Memorial at Wuustwezel on 17 June 1986.

Three days after the 1/4 KOYLI's attacked east of Esschen, 24/26 October 1944, the Hallamshires (York and Lancs) and 1st Leicesters attacked Roosendaal. The leading company of the 1/4 KOYLI passed through Roosendaal at 9 a.m. on 30 October, with the population appearing quite unconcerned. (IWM)

The Regimental history described how the people of Roosendaal lined the streets and orange flags appeared everywhere. Cpl G. Shaw (left) and Pte A. Moseley (right) joined in the celebrations, but by afternoon the Battalion had passed through and concentrated beyond the town. (IWM)

Clearing the estuary of the River Scheldt had been a difficult, dangerous and time-consuming task for the Polar Bear Division, (49th West Riding) but they soon moved on. From Roosendaal the 1/4 KOYLI moved north to capture Klundert, 6 November 1944. (IWM)

The 1/4 KOYLI spent the winter months of 1944/45 on the 'Island', the often waterlogged stretch of land between Nijmegen and Arnhem. The signals section is laying cable in a flooded area near the village of Elst, 2 March 1945. Left to right: Pte Hunt, Pte Hannah, Pte Winterbottom, Pte Elliott, Cpl Shepherd, Sgt Parkinson. (Courtesy of *Yorkshire Post*)

A fighting patrol from 'A' Company, 1/4 KOYLI, which killed one German and captured ten others in 'Operation Lark', south of Driel, February 1945. Left to right: Cpl Barnett, L/Cpl Payne, Pte Durham, Cpl Edwards, Pte McDonald, Pte Hislop, Pte Lees, Pte Hallam, L/Cpl Rain, Pte Ayrey. Ptes Lees and Durham were killed a few weeks later on 14 April 1945. (IWM)

In the 'Lark' patrol Cpl Edwards used this Piat anti-tank gun to fire two bombs into a house containing the enemy. After a brisk exchange of fire the patrol sent ten prisoners back over the 3,000 yards of flood waters to Battalion HQ. Cpl Edwards was later awarded the MM for his part in the operation. (IWM)

From 28 March onwards the Allies were secure in their positions across the Rhine. The 1/4 KOYLI, seen here after crossing the River Ijssel, 13 April 1945, joined in the attack on Arnhem the next day. (NAC (National Archive of Canada)/PA132606)

Officers and men of the 1/4 KOYLI leaving their amphibious transports after crossing the Ijssel. The officer in the centre, with the binoculars, is Frans Meijjer, a Dutch liaison officer. (NAC/PA132608)

A Casualty Clearing Station group of the 146th Brigade Field Ambulance RAMC preparing to cross the Ijssel on 13 April 1945. (NAC/PA132612)

The Regimental History records, 'Arnhem soon fell and the heroic defeat of seven months before was finally avenged.' The 1/4 KOYLI moved on to Westervoort where these prisoners, guarded by a Pte of the 1/4 KOYLI, were captured. (NAC/PA115706)

The 94th LAA Regiment (8th KOYLI) was attached to the Guards Armoured Division from Normandy to the Elbe. To uphold the light infantry tradition the RA cap badges have green backings, and the officers and senior NCOs are wearing whistle-cords.

The 1st KOYLI fired its last shots of the war at Potrau on the Elbe-Lubeck Canal, Germany. It moved to Wolfenbüttel and celebrated Minden Day in that town, the first time a Minden Regiment had ever done so. Here the 1st KOYLI is being inspected by Brig Morgan DSO MC.

Five

1945-1968

The Freedom of the City of Leeds was granted to the King's Own Yorkshire Light Infantry on 7 June 1945. This was given 'In appreciation of the glorious traditions created by the KOYLI over many years of loyal and devoted service to King and country, and in recognition of its long association with Leeds, where it was raised in 1755.' (Courtesy of *Yorkshire Post*)

Present at the ceremony in Leeds were three VCs from the First World War. Left to right: Capt. W. Edwards, Sgt J.W. Ormsby MM, Sgt L. Calvert MM. On the extreme right is Mrs C. Ward, widow of Pte Charles Ward who won the Regiment's first VC awarded during the Boer War. (Courtesy of *Yorkshire Post*)

The Guard of Honour drawn from the 6th Holding Battalion KOYLI leaving Victoria Square, Leeds, after the Freedom Ceremony. (Courtesy of *Yorkshire Post*)

The Memorial on the Battlefield of Minden. It was fitting that the 1st KOYLI should end its war here where the Regiment had gained such great distinction in the early days of its long history. The four infantry battalions of the KOYLI had 1,218 officers and men killed during the Second World War, but it is not possible to give the total KOYLI killed since many men were transferred to the Royal Artillery, Royal Armoured Corps and the Parachute Regiment.

The 1st KOYLI was stationed in Gneisenau Barracks, Minden, on 1st August 1946 and was able to have its Minden Day Parade in Minden for the second successive year.

'Z' Garrison Police Company Vienna, KOYLI, was formed in June 1946 from members of the 1/4 KOYLI. This company was attached to the Corps of Military Police and acted mainly as railway policemen in Vienna.

The 4th KOYLI's 1947 Minden Day Parade took place in York and was attended by the Colonel-in-Chief of the Regiment, Her Majesty Queen Elizabeth.

On her arrival in York, Her Majesty inspected a Guard of Honour provided by the 4th KOYLI. At Strensall Barracks she presented the Battalion with their new colours.

CSM J.P. Howson MM, Yeoman Warder. As a corporal in the 2nd KOYLI he took part in the retreat through Burma, in 1942, when his courage and initiative proved invaluable. After the action at Yenangyaung he was evacuated to Maymyo with malaria, but five days later volunteered to join a commando group operating behind enemy lines. The only one of his group to survive the operation, CSM Howson eventually made his way back to safety after enduring great hardship and almost falling into enemy hands. He spent two months in hospital recovering from malaria and dysentery.

In the spring of 1948 the 1st and 2nd KOYLI were disbanded and a new 1st KOYLI (51st-105th) was formed. A small cadre from the 1st Battalion joined the 2nd in Penang, Malaya, under the command of Lt-Col. A.B. Brown, who had lost an arm in the fighting in Normandy in 1944.

The 1st KOYLI was involved in operations against communist terrorists in Malaya. Pte Edwards (left) and Pte Chase (right) of No. 9 Platoon, found this wanted 'bandit' hiding in the undergrowth near Papan in November 1948.

No. 11 Platoon, 'D' Company, before going into action at Karagan, Malaya, 11 January 1949. It must not be forgotten that many of these soldiers were National Servicemen who were conscripted into the army at the age of eighteen and served for two years.

Men of the KOYLI on a train bound for Alor Star, Malaya, July 1949. Trains like this were sometimes ambushed and wrecked by explosives placed on or near the tracks. The trucks offered little protection, but it was possible to leave the train and deploy quite quickly.

The Queen continued to pay frequent visits to her Regiment and is seen here taking the salute with Lt Gen Sir Harold Redman at Strensall Barracks, York, in 1951. The Regimental badge can be seen in a prominent position in her hat.

In 1953 the 1st KOYLI was in Berlin where it was assigned duties at Spandau Prison, one of whose inmates was Hitler's deputy, Rudolf Hess. Here the Battalion is taking over guard duties at Spandau from a detachment of the United States Army.

The Regimental Bicentenary was celebrated in York in 1955. The Colonel-in-Chief inspected a Guard of Honour made up of fifty recruits, under the command of Capt. A.G. Thomson, which was drawn up outside the Minster.

The Colour Party on the steps of the south door of the Minster.

The Queen with the Colonel of the Regiment, Lt-Gen. Sir Harold Redman KCB CBE, make their way towards a fun-fair which was held on the cricket ground.

Before leaving the outdoor festivities the Queen accepted a bouquet of white roses from Miss Selina Slingsby, daughter of Maj. W.L. Slingsby.

Throughout its history many sons have followed their fathers into the Regiment. Probably the most outstanding example of this family link was begun by General Sir Charles Deedes KCB CMG DSO who was commissioned into the KOYLI on 11 February 1899 and was Colonel of the Regiment from 1927 to 1947. Sir Charles took part in the Boer War and was on the staff of the GHQ, British Expeditionary Force, when it went to France in August 1914. During the war he held a number of posts including GSO 2 at XIV Corps HQ, and GSO 1 at the War Office. From 1934 until 1937 he was Military Secretary to the Secretary of State for War.

Major-General C.J. Deedes CB OBE MC was commissioned into the KOYLI on 31 August 1933. When the Second World War began he was Adjutant of the 1st KOYLI and served with it in France, Norway and Italy where he was wounded twice and awarded the MC. He commanded the 1st Battalion KOYLI from June 1955 to July 1957, was appointed Deputy Director – Staff Duties in 1962 and was Chief of Staff at the HQ of Eastern Command between 1965 and 1968. Maj.-Gen. Deedes was the last Colonel of the KOYLI (1966-1968).

Major C.M.J. Deedes was commissioned into the KOYLI on 22 December 1961. He became Adjutant of the 1st KOYLI, passed Staff College and served in Malaya, Borneo, Aden, Cyprus and Germany and served on the staff of the Ministry of Defence in London for many years. At present, 1999, he is the Regimental Secretary of the KOYLI and the Light Infantry in Yorkshire.

Lt-Col. C.G. Deedes was commissioned into the KOYLI on 20 December 1963. He too passed Staff College and served with the KOYLI in Malaya and Aden. He was on the staff of the Junior Division at Staff College, and became Officer Commanding the Northern Ireland Training Team. He commanded a company of the Light Infantry and between 1986 and 1989 he set up the 8th Battalion of the Light Infantry. Lt-Col. Deedes retired in 1991.

In 1954/55 the 1st KOYLI served in Kenya and was involved in internal security duties against Mau Mau terrorists. Men of the 1st KOYLI are seen here taking time out for a brew-up on the slopes of Mount Kenya.

On leave near White Hunter's farm in the Kenya Highlands, these men of the 1st KOYLI are, left to right: Cpl P. Stainsby, Pte K. Pickering, Pte E. Cowell Pte J. Morrison. They met the Hollywood actress Rhonda Fleming who was there making the film *Odongo*.

Sometime during this tour the Regimental Buglers paid a visit to Addis Abbaba where they were inspected by the Emperor of Ethiopia, Haillie Selassie.

When the rest of the Battalion moved to Kenya, 'D' Company was sent to Cyprus where civil unrest and terrorist activity required curfews to be enforced. CSM F. Dolby MM is seen on curfew patrol sometime during 1956.

Field Marshall Sir John Harding, Governor General of Cyprus, accompanied by Major F.W. Cook, talks to the NCOs and men of 'D' Company in March 1956.

In August 1956 a temporary truce was agreed in Cyprus, which allowed these men of 'D' Company, 1st KOYLI, to remove some of the barbed wire barriers which had been erected.

Returning to England, and a short stay in York, the 1st KOYLI left for Hilden, Germany, on 30 December 1957. A shilling a day? – not for these men leaving Pay Parade at Hilden, August 1958. Left to right: Pte Clarks, Pte O'Donnell, Pte Sanderson, Pte Scott, Cpl Gale.

On an inspection tour of Germany, His Royal Highness The Duke of Gloucester visited the 1st KOYLI at Hilden, 24 March 1959. The Quarter Guard, shown here being inspected by His Royal Highness, was formed by men of 'B' Company.

While 'A' company (left to right: Pte Riddiough, Cpl Pearson, Pte Stocks) was helping in the flooded town of Hilden, August 1961, the local bank alarm went off and armed police surrounded the building. The unarmed company was 'volunteered' to cordon off half the town, but the incident ended when it was realised that water had short-circuited the alarm system.

1st KOYLI Buglers practising in the woods near Hilden under the direction of Bugle-Major Wicks, 1961. In former times the buglers were the communications branch of the Battalion and each Light Infantryman was expected to know how to respond to the various bugle calls.

As they left the barracks at Hilden, Germany, 10 July 1961, the last National Servicemen of the KOYLI returned the farewell salute given by an all-regular Guard of Honour.

The 1st KOYLI returned to the Depot at Pontefract in September 1961 and was visited by Her Majesty the Colonel-in-Chief, 28 October. Here, escorted by Capt. J.S. Cowley and Lt-Col. S.N. Floyer-Acland, Her Majesty is speaking to C/Sgt McLung.

The 1st KOYLI were not in England long because, in December 1961, they sailed for Malaya. New equipment was introduced for use in the Far East, but the design of the spade would have been familiar to many who had served with the Regiment over the previous 200 years.

Her Majesty, The Queen Mother, presented these new colours to the 4th KOYLI at the Battalion's Pontefract Barracks on 3 August 1962.

The 4th KOYLI at their annual camp, Garelochhead, Dumbartonshire, 1963. This type of camp was a far cry from those experienced by members of the Territorial battalions before the First World War.

Exercises at the Territorial's 1963 camp came under the close scrutiny of, left to right: Lt-Col. M.A.C.P. Kaye, Lt-Col. A.R. Wilson and Lt-Gen. Sir Rodger Bower. Lt-Gen.

While the 1st KOYLI was stationed in Malaya, 1964, problems occurred in nearby Brunei which needed the attention of the British Army. Part of the 1st KOYLI disembark from a train in Tampin en route for Brunei. (IWM)

Once in Brunei the men were housed in local accommodation, which meant a longhouse. The wide bamboo street outside this house appears to lead straight into the dark depths of the jungle.

Operations in the jungle sometimes necessitated movement by air. The men of 'A' Company are seen at Bareo, Sarawak, from where both helicopters and fixed wing aircraft could operate. (IWM)

The Regiment's history is filled with operations in the jungles of the Far East. This 1964 image of a jungle patrol can only differ from one in the Second Burmese War (1852-54) by the change in the men's uniforms and weapons. The jungle never changes. (IWM)

Following their tour of duty in Malaya the 1st KOYLI returned for a short time to Lucknow Barracks, Tidworth, where it was visited by the Colonel-in-Chief on 14 April 1965. The Yeoman Warder on duty in this photograph is the KOYLI veteran, CSM J.P. Howson MM.

Her Majesty always takes time to renew acquaintances with veterans. Here she is talking with Maj. Wilfred Edwards VC, and other members of the Regimental Association who were also on parade at Tidworth.

The first overseas posting for the 105th KOLI had been to Aden, in 1872, and in 1965 Aden was to be the 1st KOYLI's last posting east of Suez. The Battalion was immediately involved in internal security tasks and Pte Smith, 'A' Company, is seen guarding a snap mobile patrol in Aden town.

A searchlight and trailer were landed by helicopter on the highest building overlooking the streets of Maalla below.

In February 1966 the Battalion moved out of Aden town into the Radfan, an area very much resembling parts of the North-West Frontier near the Khyber Pass. The type of hills behind this patrol would have been all too familiar to men of the old 51st-105th.

'D' Company, 1st KOYLI, was given a mobile role and some of them are seen here, with L/Cpl Loveday in the foreground, waiting to fly in to the base at Habilayn, Aden 1966.

A 24-hour exercise for the young soldiers of the 4th KOYLI at Hornsea, July 1967, was watched by James Boyden MP, Under Secretary of State for Defence. Afterwards Mr Boyden, accompanied by the CO, Lt-Col. S.McL. Richardson, spoke to members of the training company.

The 1st KOYLI returned to Berlin in 1967 for what was to be its final foreign tour. Local geography, and a different language, did little to help the exercises in Germany where both seem to be puzzling this infantryman on exercise 'Mountain Greenery'.

Foreign tours provided some advantages and here Pte Geoffrey Gott (left) and Pte Arthur Spink, 1st KOYLI, viewed the section of the Berlin Wall near the Brandenburg Gate. The sign warned 'You are now leaving West Berlin'.

The 1st KOYLI was able to view parts of Berlin which were unavailable to the general public. Pte Matthews is driving one of the Reconnaissance platoon's Ferret scout cars on a stretch of the border road while Pte Lloyd admires the scenery.

A Guard of Honour from 'D' company, 1st KOYLI, commanded by Capt. Wilcocks, is formed up for inspection by General de Division Huchet de Guenetain, the new French Commandant, 1967.

A NATO presence was maintained in Germany from 1945 until the end of the Cold War. Pte Thompson, 1st KOYLI, in an ambush position during a night exercise, exemplified the constant need for vigilance and training.

On 1 April 1967 the 4th KOYLI (TA) underwent a name change. Their CO, Lt-Col. S.McL. Richardson wrote, 'We now become the 4th (Territorial) Battalion, the King's Own Yorkshire Light Infantry. We are already the strongest Territorial Infantry Battalion in Yorkshire; we will continue to be the best.'

The 1st KOYLI marching past the dais in the Allied Forces Day Parade, Berlin, 18 May 1968. This was to be one of the last public parades of the 1st KOYLI. On 10 July 1968 the Regiment was amalgamated with the other light infantry regiments and became the 2nd Battalion, Light Infantry Brigade.

Her Majesty Queen Elizabeth, The Queen Mother, Colonel-in-Chief of the King's Own Yorkshire Light Infantry since 1927, pictured next to the portrait of herself which was commissioned by the Regiment from the artist Oswald Birley.

The Regimental Colours and Silver of the 1st Battalion of The King's Own Yorkshire Light Infantry.